FOOTBALL AGENT
EDUCATION

FOOTBALL AGENT EDUCATION

How to Become a Football Agent:
The Guide

Dr Erkut Sögüt LL.M.,
Jack Pentol-Levy, Charlie Pentol-Levy

Matador
9 Priory Business Park,
Wistow Road, Kibworth Beauchamp,
Leicestershire. LE8 0RX
Tel: 0116 279 2299
Email: books@troubador.co.uk
Web: www.troubador.co.uk/matador
Twitter: @matadorbooks

ISBN 978 1789014 396

British Library Cataloguing in Publication Data.
A catalogue record for this book is available from the British Library.

Printed and bound by CPI Group (UK) Ltd, Croydon, CR0 4YY
Typeset in 11pt Cambria by Troubador Publishing Ltd, Leicester, UK

Matador is an imprint of Troubador Publishing Ltd

In recognition of all your help and continued support…

Ilhan Gündoğan

With special thanks to…

Yago Rama López
Nassim Touihri
Harun Arslan
Ingo Haspel
Daniel Geey
David Jackett
Rory Smith
Jörg Neubauer
Pere Guardiola
Marco Vittorio Tieghi
Edoardo Revello
Güllü Sögüt

CONTENTS PAGE

INTRODUCTION

There's no hiding that, in general, football agents (or intermediaries as they are also called) have a bad reputation in society. They are often characterised as greedy businesspeople that simply make a living based on the talent of another individual. Not only is such an opinion unjustified and untrue, but also more importantly it mustn't deter you from pursuing a career in this growing profession. Whilst this book aims to educate you on how to become a successful football agent, it additionally hopes to go some way in getting rid of the aforementioned perception. Football agency is in many ways just like any other type of business or service – you act in order to secure the best possible deals for yourself and more significantly, your client.

The book has been split up into a total of eleven chapters, each containing a varying number of sub-headings in order to give you specific details. By breaking the chapters down into smaller sections, it can also allow you to look up a particular element of football agency with relative ease at a later date. It is hoped that this contributes to a book that is accessible to everyone, at any time.

It is obvious that football agency inherently relies on the game of football and its developments. Living in a more interconnected world has meant that the sport has become far more international and increasingly globalised – consequently the agency sphere reflects this. That is why there is a continual emphasis throughout the book to give you information that is pertinent to seven of the most popular footballing associations in the world, as well as presenting the regulations made by FIFA (Fédération Internationale de Football Association). Closely linked with the internationality of football is the eclectic mix of backgrounds, ages and locations of football agents. This again has resulted in the book attempting to constantly provide information that is relevant to a global audience – and remember, a football agent is *no* specific type of person – this profession is by no means restricted to any gender, age group or environment.

To give you the best possible insight into the profession, each chapter is ended with an 'expert opinion'. This is an industry specialist relevant to the content of the chapter commenting with their experiences and thoughts on the subject, adding a personal touch and also providing you with skills, practical knowledge and wisdom that you can take with you on your journey as a football agent. These views are *not* solely given by agents, with opinions also coming from those based in professions such as law and journalism. This therefore showcases how the agency business is not exclusive – you must work closely alongside other vocations to produce the best possible results.

As previously mentioned, the book hopes to inform you about how to become a successful and morally correct football agent. Yet at the same time, reading this book alone will not ensure success in this tough industry. Being continuously active in establishing a network and always working hard and efficiently are characteristics that you *must* possess. Combined, all these elements will give you the best chance in this difficult, yet intriguing and financially rewarding profession.

CHAPTER ONE

REGISTERING AS AN AGENT

Intro

Although it is often thought that becoming a football agent is difficult, the process is simple when following the key and necessary steps. Throughout the years, football's main governing body (FIFA) have changed the rules regarding intermediary registration several times, but the 2015 FIFA Regulations on Working with Intermediaries are the most relevant for agents looking to get licensed today. Whilst FIFA have their own set of rules that they require a potential intermediary to follow, much power lies with the individual country's football association, as each nation has their own set of rules to be adhered to. This chapter shall explore the regulations and requirements for some of the main footballing federations, all of which have slightly different procedures. All of the necessary rules for registering as an intermediary (in any country) can also be found by reading the relevant association's rules on their website.

FIFA
(Fédération Internationale de Football Association)

As explained, the FIFA rules of 2015 regarding football intermediaries must be followed closely, and in conjunction with the footballing association which you are part of. FIFA mentions the following requirements:

1. Any 'natural person' (individual human being) must have an impeccable reputation and sign the 'Intermediary Declaration for Natural Persons';
2. Any 'legal person' (private or public organisation) must have an impeccable reputation and sign the 'Intermediary Declaration for Legal Persons';
3. Intermediaries are to have no contractual relationship with leagues, associations, confederations or FIFA that could lead to a potential conflict of interests;
4. The contract of representation (between an intermediary and club or player) must be authenticated by the association.

England
(FA – Football Association)

The process to become a licensed agent in England is most certainly one of the easiest amongst the large footballing nations. All that is required is an initial £500 joining fee, a renewal fee of £250 each year and proof that you do not have a criminal record, in accordance with the 'Test of Good Character and Reputation'. Finally, you must prove that you are not employed by any club and do not have any shares in a club within England.

Germany
(DFB – Deutscher Fußball-Bund)

Registering as an agent under the guidelines of the DFB is simple, yet there are different levels of registration. As a basic intermediary, all that is needed is the completed application form (as found on their website), a €500 fee which you are notified about via an invoice from the DFB accountancy department and a signature to declare that you have no contractual ties with other associations that could lead to a conflict of interests. The DFB also offers pre-registration. Although the signing up process is very similar (application form, €500 fee and signed declaration document) the main difference is that the club (or player) isn't legally obliged to ensure that the intermediary is registered, whereas they would have to provide evidence that they are officially an agent if they are only 'registered' instead of 'pre-registered'.

France
(FFF – Fédération Française De Football)

The French Football Association updated its rules and regulations for registering as an intermediary in 2011. There are now two principal examinations that you are required to take, each comprising of twenty questions. The first exam tests your legal knowledge, knowledge of tax as well as insurance and includes a case study or practical question at the end. The second examination is more specific to the world of football. Candidates are questioned on the football rules and regulations in France as well as internationally.

Spain
(RFEF – Real Federación Española de Fútbol)

The enrolment process in Spain is vastly different to the other leagues. Firstly, an applicant must submit a written application to the General Secretariat of the RFEF, and if this request is accepted, the candidate will be summoned to interview (which can be conducted via a web-video service). After passing the interview, the rest of the procedure resembles many other associations. Each aspiring intermediary must have an impeccable reputation as well as pay the obligatory fee to the RFEF and sign the 'Code of Conduct' forms.

Italy
(FIGC – Federazione Italiana Giuoco Calcio)

Unlike Spain, the method to becoming a registered agent is simple, and it greatly resembles the other associations. In addition to the declaration of 'professional fairness', one must not have committed sports fraud or have a criminal record. Furthermore, there is to be a payment to the FIGC that is valid for one year, after which it is required (if wanted) to re-register via a fast-track process (unless any amendments have to be added to the aforementioned declaration). Alternatively, an intermediary may register before the FIGC only in the event of a specific representation contract's filing.

As of very recently, there has been an important addition to the rules in Italy. Now, an agent must pass a qualifying exam in order to be a fully licensed intermediary.

Portugal
(FPF – Federação Portuguesa de Futebol):

The Portuguese footballing body has implemented a straightforward process to becoming a registered agent. Along with the relevant identification documents, those wanting to become a registered intermediary have to send in proof of no criminal acts being committed as well as a declaration of solvency and a confirmation of no other contracts that could lead to a conflict of interests. In addition to the FPF focusing on the finances of a potential agent (an applicant is also required to have a civil liability insurance policy and a regularised tax situation), the association is keen on agents having a good reputation, which is frequently re-assessed.

United States of America
(USSF – United States Soccer Federation)

The registration process for becoming an agent in the United States is very similar to that of England. To go along with the completed Intermediary Registration Form, an initial $400 must be paid to the governing body and then a renewal fee of $50 each year. Moreover, you are subject to a background check and must not be employed by FIFA, or any other governing body or national association. The USSF (much like the German association) also offers pre-registration, which entitles you to the same benefits in increasing efficiency in transfers and contracts.

Summary

- Making sure that you are legally registered as an agent in the appropriate association is key, and there are harsh implications if the rules are not abided by.
- If you are the agent of a player transferring to another country, you may **or** may not have to register as an intermediary in the new country as well – this depends on the exact rules set out by each federation.
- For additional information on the associations already mentioned, as well as details on registering in other countries, visit the website of the relevant federation.

The expert's view – Yago Rama López (Sports lawyer and football consultant)

"Based on FIFA regulations, registering has always been the first step in becoming a football agent. In 1994, FIFA regulated the work of agents with the PAR (Players' Agents Regulations), and from here started the process of regularly developing the rules. For instance, in the 2008 edition of PAR, FIFA changed the role of national associations in the process of regulating intermediaries. This change saw each country now having to implement and enforce the standard FIFA regulations, as well as creating their own individual rules that respect the national law applicable in the territory of the association.

"However, in 2015, FIFA decided to completely alter the rules, and the FIFA Regulations on Working with Intermediaries removed the old regulations on agent accreditation and quality standards. Here, the objective of the new rulebook changed – it was no longer to regulate access to the activity of players' agents (now officially 'intermediaries'), but to orientate this activity for better control, establishing minimum standards and requirements together with a transparent registration system. In the 2015 regulations, FIFA also determined that there should not be any payments involving minors, and considers legal persons/companies as official intermediaries themselves. In general, the registration requirements for agents with the national associations do in fact carry legal uncertainties and ambiguities that will at some point be better clarified by football's governing bodies, various courts and also the EU Commission.

"As a registered intermediary in different countries, it is interesting to note the differences between federations. As described in this chapter, becoming an agent in England (FA – Football Association) was simpler than the process I went through in Switzerland (SFV – Schweizerischer Fussballverband). Here, an intermediary must set up a company and is therefore subject to the same rules as any other employment agency. Consequently, you can't be registered if you don't have a residence or work permit.

"Stemming from this, you may ask yourself if it

is necessary for an intermediary to register in **all** the associations in order to carry out the profession effectively. There is no right or wrong answer to this question; you just have to find the solution that works best for you. But personally, I don't think it is essential to register with lots of associations when beginning as an agent. As a starting point, I would advise you to be registered at **your** national association or wherever you think your work will take place. From here, you can officially start your career as a football agent!"

CHAPTER TWO

GETTING INTO THE BUSINESS

Intro

For aspiring agents, often the most difficult aspect is how to get into the business and become an established intermediary. It should be known that there is no set method that you have to follow, as leading football agents all have different backgrounds and stories that led to them entering their profession. As a result, it is difficult to formulate a precise guide. Nevertheless, there are of course some more common routes into the football business that will be discussed in this chapter. If you do not find yourself in one of these categories, it does not diminish your chances of becoming a successful agent, as there are still many other ways into this profession!

Internship or direct job application

A common way into the footballing business is through applying for an internship or job, either towards the end of your studies, or after completing them. The most suitable type of companies would be sports agencies themselves, and it is important to remember that gaining experience in either the marketing or legal department of these firms can prove to be just as valuable in the long term as working immediately alongside an agent. It is essential that during your time at any of these agencies, you try as hard as you can to grow and enhance your network and contacts in order to acquire as much knowledge as possible. It may be the case that the contacts you make during your time at these companies turn out to be crucial in your future career in the business.

A contact in the industry

Knowing somebody who is already connected to the footballing business is another frequent method used by aspiring intermediaries. A connection who is already established in the sporting world could range from a club employee (like a manager or sporting director) to an existing agent or even a player. This area of entry into football is perhaps where the bad perception of intermediaries stems from, as it is sometimes (although not always) the case that a club employee, often a sporting director, is disingenuous. The director may instruct an up-and-coming intermediary about the players that the club is interested in, so the agent could get a mandate for the player, and enable all parties to make money. Although this isn't totally legitimate, it **does** occur, and it is legal. Nevertheless, knowing someone who works within the sport (in whatever capacity) is certainly a great way into the profession.

Family member or friend

Another method to become more involved in the business is if a family member is an emerging talent or even a professional footballer. Regarding having a relationship with an upcoming player, it is crucial for a potential intermediary to not only follow the strict rules (see Chapter 1 and Chapter 8), but to offer support and advice to help the player in making the right choices on their journey to becoming a professional footballer. Moreover, a friend can also play a key role in a footballer's career once they are established, especially in helping manage their everyday affairs. This is particularly the case when the actual agent has multiple clients or lives in a different country, and as a result, friends will sort out minor issues and help with organising the player's daily routine. Consequently, it is significant for the intermediary to work alongside players' friends to ensure that they can truly benefit. In addition, it is not uncommon for a friend of a player to become their agent too, as often they are genuinely trusted. This can allow the friend to launch their own agency and expand their clientele. This business model was used by Nassim Touihri (the agent of Lukas Podolski), as he formed Fair Play Career Management and took his friend Podolski with him to his new firm.

The following table demonstrates some well-known examples of a family member representing a player. Despite the rarity of having a relative as a professional footballer, you mustn't feel discouraged – in the majority of cases, although the family member will be the listed agent, they will still receive help and advice from qualified and educated agents behind the scenes.

Player/ manager	Country	Agent	Agent–client relation
Sergio Ramos	Spain	René Ramos	Brother
Sami Khedira	Germany	Denny Khedira	Brother
Danny Welbeck	England	Chris/Wayne Welbeck	Brothers
Diego Simeone	Argentina	Natalia Simeone	Sister
Mats Hummels	Germany	Hermann Hummels	Father
Mario Götze	Germany	Jürgen Götze	Father
Lionel Messi	Argentina	Jorge Horacio Messi	Father
Álvaro Morata	Spain	Alfonso Morata	Father
Arjen Robben	Netherlands	Hans Robben	Father
Mauro Icardi	Argentina	Wanda Nara	Wife

General business person

Many successful agents start off in mainstream professions, perhaps specialising in areas such as law, banking or teaching. Jobs like these, as well as so many others, are a great way into the world of sports as a player (and their representatives at the time) will always need the advice of specialists, for example in legal or financial matters. Consequently, there will be countless opportunities for professionals to make their way into the world of sport. This was the case with Jörg Neubauer, who started his career as a lawyer but turned into a prolific football agent, currently representing those such as Leon Goretzka and Kevin Trapp.

However, the legal profession is not alone in breeding intermediaries. Spielerrat, the company who represent Per Mertesacker, was formed by three friends who previously worked at Adidas and decided to become football agents, with a strong network having been created as a result of their previous jobs. Furthermore, there are many business people that work closely with sport, whilst not actually being agents. Often, a business person can take care of a player's sponsorships or commercial dealings (or at least give advice on this subject) while continuing their day-to-day profession. Therefore, it is clear that there are numerous routes in the world of sports agency, with some ending in becoming an actual agent and others that just involve advice.

Buying an agency

Perhaps the least common (and most expensive way) to get into the footballing business is to buy an existing and established agency. Although this is fairly rare, an example of such a takeover is not difficult to find in recent news. In 2016, Chinese company Wuhan Double Co. Ltd. purchased the sports agency Nice International Sports Limited, in a deal that also involved a partnership with Pere Guardiola's firm, Media Base Sports. This is of course an extremely costly way into the industry, however it is highly effective and efficient if the funds are available. Furthermore, despite it seeming unrealistic for many, if one was to get a job or internship at a large firm outside of the footballing business, a merger or deal with a football agency is not totally impractical.

Summary

- The most important thing to remember is that there is no correct or incorrect way to become a football agent, as the top intermediaries come from all sorts of different backgrounds.
- If you are a student or young professional, getting experience through an internship at an agency can provide you with great insight and start your vital network in the business.
- For those already established in another profession, the world of football is within reach, as so many other industries such as law and finance have links to the sport.

The expert's view – Dr Erkut Sögüt (Agent of Mesut Özil)

"My journey to becoming an agent started in my third year of university. As a law student coming to the end of my degree, I contacted the company of Harun Arslan who was, and still is, the agent of Joachim Löw. I was able to get in touch with his firm (ARP Sportmarketing) through his secretary, who I knew. A brief five-minute meeting with Harun was like nothing I had ever experienced before. After each question I posed, he kept reiterating how he employs nobody, not even interns. Before leaving, I told him that I wanted to create a monthly magazine that covered five topics of football agency, and from that moment I worked on this project every weekend in conjunction with my law degree.

"Around six months later, Harun (knowing that I studied law) asked for advice regarding a case with the Turkish Football Federation (TFF). With much work and effort, I won the case for him and cleared all the legal troubles. Since then, he has told me that the door of his agency will always be open! So, for me the path to becoming a football agent was **not** easy – yet with hard work and belief, anything can be achieved."

CHAPTER THREE

THE WORK OF A FOOTBALL AGENT

Intro

Despite there being a certain perception that the football agent profession is simple and straightforward, it is a job that requires you to be active all the time and encompasses different tasks each and every day. Like nearly all careers, the busier you are the better, as more work correlates to more clients and thus more income! There is no fixed daily routine for a football agent, although intermediaries working for an agency **will** have more structure, but even so life in this profession is unpredictable and exciting.

Match days

Arguably the most significant part of the week is the match day of your client(s). Depending on the exact nature of your relationship with the player, motivational conversations before the game can be greatly beneficial, and given the importance of your client's performance in aiding your job, every little to help them has to be done. Regarding the logistics of the match day, most players normally have an allocation of two tickets, although it is becoming more and more common for players to have access to a box. This would normally come in the form of their own suite, as evidenced at Manchester City, where the Colin Bell Stand is home to ten squad-member boxes including Raheem Sterling, John Stones and club captain Vincent Kompany.

However, these private areas can also be shared between players. This can be found at Arsenal, with Santi Cazorla and Nacho Monreal having joint ownership over their box. In either case, as the agent, it would be your responsibility to organise the guests. Whilst some family members of the player will request access to the tickets, it is crucial to find the balance between them and business guests. Allocating the tickets between friends, family, commercial partners, potential partners and other agents in the business is key. To help with this, you should always keep in mind that it is your job and you are in the business side of football; try to treat these match days as potential gateways to further deals.

Location of work

Being a football agent is a job that requires you to be active and thus normally involves much travelling. As already mentioned, those working as part of an agency will certainly have more structure to their routines, and consequently would have a desk or office to be based from. However, for those that are independent of a firm, your headquarters are everywhere and change every day! Interaction with your client is key, and therefore visiting them at either their house or the training ground, as well as accompanying them to commercial shootings, is of paramount importance. Most agents will have a certain location in which they prefer to meet business people and other agents. Sometimes a low-key restaurant or café can provide the perfect setting to talk over deals, but additionally upscale hotels or eateries are also popular amongst intermediaries, particularly when hosting significant or foreign guests. Therefore, it is clear that like most aspects of the business, there is really no set or fixed formula and it greatly depends on you as an individual and the situation you find yourself in.

Going to work

The most important thing to remember when working as a football agent is to always be prepared. Your day will mostly comprise of meetings with a range of different people, perhaps spanning various industries, and therefore it is for you to be ready for the day ahead. This includes being equipped with a phone and laptop (with chargers) as well as a notepad. Keeping a copy, either digitally or in writing, of what has been agreed in your meetings helps you keep track of all your business. As with any profession, preparation and organisation are key factors in success.

Networking

The ability to network is an absolutely fundamental requirement of a successful football agent. This skill comprises of two main elements – the creation of a vast network, and the subsequent exploitation of the network in order to benefit yourself and your client. Whilst building a wide-reaching network may seem like a daunting task, it is *all* about using already established contacts to introduce you to others, and repaying these favours in whatever way you can.

Similarly, introducing two contacts of your own will earn you respect and a 'good name' within the industry. To have a strong network, it requires you to keep in touch with everyone, even when there doesn't seem to be a need to. This could be done by communicative methods such as email, messages and phone calls, but perhaps more effectively by setting up face-to-face meetings. This can take the form of an invitation to a match day or organising a time to catch up at an office, hotel, restaurant or café. Overall, the importance of building and effectively using a network in the football agency business cannot be underestimated – it forms the basis of your everyday actions and will ensure success in this industry.

Conferences and events

Throughout the year, there are numerous events in the football business calendar that would be worthwhile for aspiring agents to attend. Whilst not all of these will specifically focus on football agency, talks on marketing and finance within the sport can still provide crucial details that a good agent requires. The most well known include Leaders in Sport and the Wyscout Forum – these events (amongst others) are well worth going to. Events tend to attract great speakers from a variety of sectors, and they can provide you with interesting and useful skills, information, and also experience.

In addition, another advantage to these conferences and events is that so many individuals in the industry are present in the same space, at the same time – a rare occurrence. It gives you the chance to meet new people and make worthwhile contacts, thereby expanding your network within a relatively short span of time. You never know when any of these new contacts could become helpful when conducting future business activities. Also, it could be the case in years to come that after establishing yourself as a top football agent, you may be invited to talk at some of these events – this would be an offer that you really shouldn't turn down.

Managing commercial relationships

To assume that the work of a football agent is solely confined to the pitch would be grossly incorrect. In fact, the bulk of an agent's work is conducted away from football stadiums, with a large part of day-to-day activities revolving around dealing with commercial deals and relationships with sponsors. Whilst this is also touched upon in Chapters 7, 9 and 11, its significance shouldn't be understated in relation to the daily routine of an agent.

Nowadays, in the current football climate, it is more than likely that your player will have (or will get) some sort of boot deal from a sports brand. Such commercial deals could inevitably lead to photoshoots and filming, in which you would be the first point of contact as the mediator between the player and the sponsor. If your player happens to share a common sponsorship with the club that they play for, it may lead to more advertising (and thus monetary) opportunities for your client – this is therefore something that has to be taken into consideration when negotiating a transfer. However, regardless of this, keeping good relations with sponsors is vital – inviting them to a game or sending them signed memorabilia can always help bolster the relationship that you and your client have with any given brand.

Summary

- Unlike most other industries, football is non-stop – you must remember that there is always work to do, and those that work hardest and smartest will succeed the most.
- Generally, work in this profession is unpredictable, and that is why flexibility (in addition to preparation and organisation) is so crucial – particularly when dealing with numerous clients or having overseas business interests.
- Despite the difficulties you may face, the fact that every day brings a new challenge to overcome is not only exciting, but also really rewarding and something you should relish.

The expert's view – Ilhan Gündoğan (Agent of Ilkay Gündoğan)

"With regards to the day-to-day work of a football agent, I know that some people believe it is so easy that anyone can do it. However, the truth is actually very far from this. The content of my job varies greatly each day and is also dependent on the time of year.

"During the season my focus is mostly towards the management of my nephew, Ilkay Gündoğan. This involves speaking to him on a regular basis, providing him with support and encouragement when necessary, as well as motivating him so that he keeps playing to the best of his ability. Moreover, I am there for anything he needs – similar to a concierge service. Finally, leading up to each match day, I coordinate with the guests that will attend the game – inviting key people in the business as well as off-the-field individuals from brands and also companies is important.

"Seeking and managing commercial deals for my player is likewise a big part of my job. This involves meeting with current partnered brands on a regular basis as well as seeking new possible endorsements. Most importantly, being available twenty-four hours a day, seven days week is something you must be prepared for if you wish to be successful in this business – because if you aren't, then somebody else will be."

CHAPTER FOUR

WORKING WITH PLAYERS

Intro

Sometimes, it can be difficult to find the correct balance between managing the business and personal side of a player's life, as the two are so often intertwined. Unfortunately, there is no set procedure about how to best work alongside a player, and it greatly depends on the age, fame and personality of your client. Nevertheless, there are certain actions that are advised when dealing directly with a player, and equally there are some things better left undone. The way in which you choose to work with a client is also impacted by your own situation. This relies on not only how many clients you have, but if those relationships are simply mandates for a transfer or full-time representation, and if you are employed by an agency or working independently.

Working with youth players

A different approach is highly recommended depending on the age of the player. For a young player, the agent should on the one hand be encouraging and nurturing their talent, whilst at the same time seeking potential sponsors and casting an eye to the future. With players that are still in school, it is partially your responsibility as the agent to make sure they continue to be educated and do school work. As a result, you may work closely with the schools and academies, as the teachers and coaches form an important part of a player's early career. Such a point is validated by how Mesut Özil, Manuel Neuer and Leroy Sané all went to the same school and later to the Schalke 04 Academy.

When dealing with young professionals looking to gain recognition, a possible method could be to find your player a small club in a lower division and hope that they work their way up. However, finding a much larger club and subsequently agreeing a loan deal is also a good way to gain experience and get exposure in the tough world of football. It is strongly suggested that the intermediary involves the parents of the player when dealing with their child's professional career, both in terms of footballing moves and sponsorship deals. Remember, it is imperative that an agent is aware of all the rules (both those of FIFA and the relevant football association) regarding the representation of minors – these can be found in Chapter 8.

Working with established professionals

With a client who is already fairly well known (something that often, but not always, comes with age), it is important for you to make the most of both their footballing ability and sponsorship potential, especially when they are at the pinnacle of their career. When dealing with an established professional, it can be really beneficial to have a long-term plan, as well as back-up plans for safety. Although football is unpredictable, making connections with a range of clubs that could in the future be a big transfer for your player is characteristic of a good agent. Regarding the personal life of your player, it is crucial to find a balance. Whilst you have their best intentions and interests at heart, being an agent who is too controlling and overbearing is not the way forward, and those who are will not last long in the business.

Working with the friends and family of a player

Despite not being thought of as truly significant, knowing how to work alongside the friends and family of your client is actually something of importance. Often, those who are close to the player are the people who can influence them the most, and therefore working with them is pivotal. Of course, this may be a legal obligation with the parents of a youth player, but even a famous footballer will always take advice from those closest to them. Consequently, as an agent, you should keep close family and friends aware of your intentions, both with the player's football career and commercial agreements.

Working with the spouse or partner of a player

A difficult situation that nearly all football agents face at some point is when their player enters a relationship. The influence of a spouse or partner is obvious in the sport, as the 'other half' of a footballer plays a crucial decision-making role. For example, the career of a player's partner may impact the likelihood of a transfer to another city or country, and often if a couple have young children, this too can make moving more difficult. Therefore, it is pivotal that you, as the agent, recognise the personal needs of your client but at the same time make sure that they are fully aware that they have to make the most of their career whilst there is the possibility to do so.

The size of your clientele

Much like how to deal with your player, it is important to find the right balance between having too many and only a few clients. Although it may seem financially beneficial to have lots of clients when starting as a football agent, it is difficult to manage numerous players at the same time, especially when fairly inexperienced as an agent yourself. Nevertheless, multiple clients tend to mean multiple sources of income, and therefore it is advised that you choose perhaps a handful of clients who have great potential. The fact that having various clients is time-consuming and fairly difficult stresses the importance of getting on with your player's family and friends, as they can help out with some of the smaller and more day-to-day tasks.

Mandate for a transfer or normal agent?

An important differentiation to make is the two main categories of representation. Whilst a typical agent takes care of the majority of a client's affairs, there is also the possibility to just have a mandate for a transfer. Depending on what exactly was agreed, a mandate means that you would handle just the player's transfer for a certain period of time (normally one transfer window) to a certain league or country where you have good connections. Consequently, you would try hard to complete a transfer whilst getting a negotiated fee from the transaction, without becoming their full-time agent.

This difference between acting with mandates and being a regular agent is fairly common in football. If an agent has a well-known client who requires much time, they could sign a mandate for the transfer of another player to provide another source of income, whilst not committing long term. However, this isn't the only reason why the mandate could be pursued. An up-and-coming agent and player may agree on a mandate for a transfer as a trial period for future representation, as it is sometimes thought of as a test of the ability of an agent.

Working for an agency

The way in which you work with a client differs greatly according to whether you are an independent agent, or an agent who is part of a large firm. If you are in fact working for an agency, it is a little less likely that you will have to deal with the more menial tasks of an agent, as there will be people in the company who would be able to take care of organising some of the less important daily aspects. Although this may seem beneficial, being part of an agency perhaps results in a less personal relationship with your client, something that is crucial to have. Nevertheless, working for a larger company brings you many things that an independent intermediary may not have themselves, like a far larger contact list which could yield great power with potential sponsors. Again, this is a decision that only you can make on your journey into the world of sports agency.

Summary

- You must always be aiming to find the appropriate balance between the business and personal aspects of your job – this is something only you can discover as you go along.
- A good way to try to ensure success is to always be open and communicate frequently with your client, as this proves to them your honesty and transparency.
- The decisions that you make with regards to clients and other aspects of the profession are without doubt important, but at the same time they are not permanent – always be sure to review and improve the choices that you have made.

The expert's view – Nassim Touihri (Managing Director, Fair Play Career Management)

"As an agent, it is crucial to have a good, strong relationship with your player. For me, this is established through trust and honesty at all times, and these are the most important characteristics of an intermediary who is successful in their field of work. Although this is easier said than done, in my experience there are ways of achieving this type of relationship with a player. You must always be willing to help them in their personal life when they come to you for advice, but at the same time, do not try to interfere in matters that simply don't concern you – finding the balance is key. Remember, not only do you have to protect your player from others, but you must also protect them from themselves, as they can endanger their own career at any point.

"Regarding the business aspect of the player-agent relationship, you have to be constantly thinking ahead to the future and making smart plans. At the end of the day, as an intermediary you are responsible for *all* of your client's interests and you have to be managing both their football career and making preparations for their post-playing career – this is the sign of a good agent.

"Personally, I was a little lucky in that Lukas Podolski has been my close friend since we were young kids at school. But at the same time, I had to work incredibly hard and my role today was not given to me because of this. Even when I did not officially represent Lukas, I was always by his side giving advice in both personal and contractual matters. Eventually, our relationship evolved into what it is today. As I said (and will always say), trust and honesty are the qualities that breed success in this business."

CHAPTER FIVE

WORKING WITH MANAGERS AND SPORTING DIRECTORS

Intro

Although this book centres around the player–agent relationship, the representation of other individuals within the sport is becoming increasingly pertinent and important. More and more top managers and sporting directors are receiving professional advice from intermediaries, with specific agencies being set up to do exactly this. For example, Project B (the company that represents manager Jürgen Klopp, amongst others) showcases this new and developing type of agency as they focus **not** on players, but those in management positions. Whilst the skills required to represent such clients are similar, there are some important differences to note.

Being the agent of a manager

Much like football players, managers need professional representation. Even though they are less likely to bring you lucrative sponsorship deals, there are still opportunities to be successful through the contracts that they sign with clubs. Whereas with football players there are strict rules and regulations on representing them, there are actually no such fixed guidelines or practices that have to be adhered to with managers. However, despite there being no fixed limit on commission, it is generally assumed that the agent is entitled to around 10 per cent as a reward for their work on negotiating the contract.

Advantages of representing a manager

In addition to the negotiated commission, there are numerous benefits as a result of being the agent of a football manager. If you represent the manager, it gives you the opportunity to utilise this important figure at the club in order to make transfers for others that you may be the agent of. This practice is one frequently resorted to by lots of agents, including Jorge Mendes. He has acted as the registered intermediary for both the player and manager in many transfer negotiations. The table on the next page details some of these occasions as all the listed players are represented by Mendes and were transferred to a club where the manager is also a client of his (José Mourinho in these examples).

By doing this, you will always have a link to the

club where the manager is at, even when they leave. Furthermore, this advantage is closely coupled with the fact that the manager (if you are their agent) can easily introduce you to other key employees at the club, which can strengthen your position if you already manage a player there. For example, if through the manager you can improve your relations with other important decision-makers, it is more likely that your player would be treated favourably, perhaps in terms of getting picked for the team or when discussing a new contract.

Player	Year	Transfer	Fee
Paulo Ferreira	2004–05	Porto → Chelsea	£18m
Tiago	2004–05	Benfica → Chelsea	£13.5m
Ricardo Carvalho	2004–05	Porto → Chelsea	£27m
Nuno Morais	2004–05	Penafiel → Chelsea	Free
Ricardo Quaresma	2008–09	Porto → Inter Milan	£22.1m
Ángel Di María	2010–11	Benfica → Real Madrid	£29.7m
Ricardo Carvalho	2010–11	Chelsea → Real Madrid	£7.2m
Fábio Coentrão	2011–12	Benfica → Real Madrid	£27m
Diego Costa	2014–15	Atlético Madrid → Chelsea	£34.2m

Source: Transfermarkt (correct as of January 2018)

Young managers

In modern football, young managers are becoming increasingly used by top clubs around the world, and therefore it is important to try and establish good links and connections with these promising coaches. Usually, young managers will start their career by taking charge of the lower youth teams (U17 or U19), and slowly work their own way to the U23 team or second team. It is often the case that when the manager of the main team is sacked or resigns, the board look to these coaches, who understand the set-up of the club so well, in order to assume responsibility for the first team. The same logic can be easily applied to the already existing assistant manager, who can also temporarily (and then permanently) fill the vacant managerial spot. Consequently, it is beneficial to have good relationships with young and promising managers, as frequently they will become the first team manager in years to come.

Working alongside a sporting director

The key advice to remember when working with a sporting director (or any club official besides the manager) is to try and get into their mind and way of thinking, and this is where your understanding of football – as well as keeping up-to-date with all news and transfers – is crucial. Using all the resources that you have, you have to try and predict what the sporting director needs for his club in terms of players. If, for example, the team have sold their starting striker or their striker gets injured, it could be clever for you to get a mandate for a striker's transfer and try to sell them to that club.

Additionally, there is another way in which an agent can work with a sporting director or a senior club official. Whilst getting a mandate for a player's transfer is common, getting a mandate from the club to conduct their transfer policy is becoming more frequent in the sport. The club would authorise you to contact potential players on their behalf, whilst you would receive an agreed commission for your services. This set-up can be found at Wolverhampton Wanderers, as Jorge Mendes became the agent for the club during the 2016 summer transfer window and has been highly influential in their successful recruitment since then. Although this relationship is known to the public, such agreements between an agent and sporting director are often kept secret so that the club doesn't have to bind themselves to the recommendations of a single intermediary.

Summary

- Although it may not seem as rewarding as being the agent of a high-profile football player, representing senior club officials can be greatly advantageous as they often open doors and allow you access to the team's transfer dealings.
- Many agents (and agencies) opt for a mix between players and club executives in order to get the benefits of being close to both types of client.
- You must always be aware of the intentions of managers and officials – they are likely to have 'closed-door' relationships with many intermediaries in the hope of getting the best possible deals for themselves.

The expert's view – Harun Arslan
(Owner, ARP Sportmarketing GmbH)

"At first glance you may think that there aren't really any significant differences between representing a player and a club employee (such as a manager, coach, or director). After all, you treat both with importance as your client, and both entail work such as contractual matters and monetary terms. Whilst this *is* correct, there are some key distinctions that should be made.

"Firstly, you have to take into consideration the age of the client. For a player (especially if they are young), the agent often takes up the role of an additional parent, whereas with a coach you ought to expect a completely different dynamic. Coaches are generally experienced personalities, and top-level managers work in a highly complex environment. A coach is expected to always stay focused, and every single word or action performed reflects on the club that they are contracted to. Although it is in the interest of the club to protect their employees, the relationship with an agent carries a special function. You act with the necessary distance to give neutral advice in all circumstances and provide clarity in difficult situations, making tough decisions easier. In many ways, the agent of a club employee is like a good friend – you are there to provide unbiased support with the best intentions.

"In addition to making sure your client gives off a 'good image' to the public, working in this area of football will subject you to important contractual and career decisions, as well as establishing a strong network to be utilised in the future. In the current game, on-pitch failure usually leads to the dismissal of coaches, managers and other club employees, thus making your job exceedingly important."

CHAPTER SIX

TRANSFER WINDOWS

Intro

For a football agent, the transfer window is arguably the busiest time. In spite of the unpredictability of the football market, the best agents will have been preparing moves for their clients long before the windows officially open, as work for all types of transfer must be started in advance. The most important thing to remember is the more effort you put into building and improving your network throughout the year, the easier it is to push a transfer over the finish line. As previously mentioned in Chapter 4, you may either be representing your client as their agent, or acting on a player's behalf due to a signed mandate – whichever is to be the case, it is important to remain professional, shrewd and effective in negotiations and discussions. Remember – it is crucial that you get your business concluded before the deadline, and as a rough guideline, some dates of popular transfer windows are detailed below.

Country	Pre-season window	Mid-season window	Record transfer (M £, M €/$)
England (FA)	9th June –31st August	1st January –31st January	Paul Pogba (£89, €105)
Germany (DFB)	1st July –31st August	1st January –31st January	Corentin Tolisso (£38, €41.5)
France (FFF)	9th June –31st August	1st January –31st January	Neymar Jr. (£200, €222)
Spain (RFEF)	1st July –1st September	1st January –31st January	Philippe Coutinho (£108, €120)
Italy (FIGC)	1st July –31st August	3rd January –31st January	Gonzalo Higuaín (£81, €90)
Portugal (FPF)	3rd July–22nd September	3rd January –2nd February	Raúl Jiménez (£20, €22)
United States of America (USSF)	14th February –18th May	10th July –9th August	Miguel Almirón, Michael Bradley (£6.7, ~$10)

Source: Transfermarkt (correct as of January 2018)

Preparation for the window

Football agents often joke that the transfer window has no start and no end. Although the dates provided give you the actual days of which transfers can be finalised, the work that goes into them starts long before the deal takes place. It is rare that any deal (even if it is completed towards the end of the window) hasn't been the subject of talks between the agent of the player and representatives of the club for weeks, if not months. Therefore, it is crucial for you to be constantly monitoring the needs of clubs in case a player you represent (or have a mandate for) fits the requirements as you see them. This research could be as easy as looking up when key players are 'out of contract' or simply knowing what teams are lacking position-wise. Transfer windows *can* often be the pinnacle of the work that you have been putting in all year round – but remember, do not rush or be forced into any deal, and always keep in close contact with clients in order to know what *they* want.

Free agents

Given the huge rise in transfer fees across the game, free agents are becoming more appealing for clubs to sign. A free agent is essentially when a player is 'out of contract', and is therefore allowed to transfer to another club without any transfer fee being paid. This method is not only appealing for prospective clubs, but for agents and players too, as you can negotiate larger wages and signing-on fees due to a lack of transfer payment. Whilst this situation is certainly beneficial, the fact that most contracts nowadays are signed on a five-year basis means that waiting for a client to be a free agent is a lengthy process that could detract from making the most out of a player's career. Nevertheless, this strategy remains popular amongst agents, with examples being illustrated in Chapter 10.

Loans

Perhaps more relevant to a client who is either young or on the fringes of the first team, loan deals can be truly advantageous if conducted correctly. A loan can vary in length and just depends on what the two clubs agree on; however, they are normally for the duration of the season (or half of a season). It is very common for the 'parent club' to ask for either a contribution to the wages of the player, or for a sum of money for the duration of the loan time. As already mentioned, from the perspective of an agent, loans can be of use. If your client is given more playing time at another club, it could showcase their potential worth for the 'parent club' in the future, or increase their transfer value if you are looking for a permanent move elsewhere.

Permanent deals

The most common method of transfer is the more straightforward permanent deal. This occurs when two clubs agree a fee for a player, which is then subject to the passing of a medical and finalising of a contract. Every step of this process requires the agent to be involved, whilst acting on behalf of your client's interests at all times. Essentially, your strategy ultimately depends on whether or not your player wants to leave the club that they are currently contracted to. If your client has asked for a move, then it becomes your prerogative to speak with the club hierarchy and start holding 'discussions' with potentially interested parties. Persuasion and negotiation become pivotal skills here, as you have to convince all sides that the decisions they are making are beneficial. If you find yourself representing a player who wishes to stay at their present club, yet other teams have come to you declaring their interest, you should still pass on these sentiments to your client. It could be the case that what they offer becomes tempting for both your player and the club that they play for.

Options to buy

The supposed middle ground between a loan and permanent deal is often deemed to be the 'option to buy clause'. This involves a club agreeing to loan a player for a certain amount of time, with an agreement also being in place for a full transfer. This strategy is becoming more common for clubs as they can test the player out, without having the obligation of a permanent deal. Recent examples of this can be found with top European players, such as James Rodríguez (Real Madrid and Bayern Munich) and Douglas Costa (Bayern Munich and Juventus). Sometimes whether or not the full transfer takes place is down to appearance and performance-based clauses that were initially agreed – these would have been made clear, and it is for you as the agent to be involved in the deal-making process. This method of transfer has also been adapted in recent transfer windows too. The agreement between Monaco and Paris Saint-Germain for Kylian Mbappé has been labelled as an 'obligation to buy' rather than an 'option to buy', with the latter club supposedly required to follow through with the deal after the loan period has come to an end. Either way, an agent must be aware about the possible use of both methods.

Contract renewals

Although the renewal of a player's contract can take place at any time of the year, they are still heavily linked to transfer windows, or more specifically the transfer activity of a potentially interested club. Transfer windows *can* provide an optimum time for agents, as interest in your client from another team can allow you to negotiate from a position of great strength rather than weakness. Additionally, if your client's club was to purchase another player on a significantly higher wage, it may give you scope to renegotiate the now inferior wage that your player finds themselves on. Whilst such tactics should be efficiently used, it shouldn't come at the cost of morality. The activity of clubs is a helpful bargaining tool, yet at the same time you would be ill-advised to hold any club hostage over this as it could give you a bad reputation within the industry.

Summary

- There is no doubt that due to the increase in money being exchanged in football you will be extremely busy in each and every transfer window, as at least one club will have some interest in your player, even if no deal is likely to come to fruition.
- One of the most pivotal things to remember is to keep in constant contact with your client — you must be fully

aware of what they want, and additionally inform them of any approaches from any club.

• Given the importance of transfers in your career, you must always think over each decision – of course you can never be totally sure, but make choices based on all the possible information and facts that you have.

The expert's view – Ingo Haspel (Owner, Haspel Sportconsulting)

"As already established, football players are only permitted to be transferred to another club during a certain period, known as the transfer window. It is also at this point where players are granted permission by the relevant governing bodies to play for their new team, and this is important to note when conducting deals *outside* the window or with an agreement for a future transfer. Depending on the confederation, different transfer windows exist. The European governing body UEFA (Union of European Football Associations) instituted two transfer periods in the season where permanent deals can be finalised. Therefore, in European countries the dates of these windows tend to end on the same day but usually differ on exact timings.

"Crucially, for a transfer to be completed, it must take place before the end of the deadline of the *buying* club. The transfer windows close precisely on the minute, and being only seconds late in providing the documents to the corresponding locations renders the transfer incomplete. Consequently, it will only be at the opening of the following transfer window that it is possible again."

CHAPTER SEVEN

CONTRACTS

Intro

Perhaps the most complex aspect of being a football agent is dealing with the contracts and negotiations on behalf of your client. Such contracts can be easily separated into two categories – those that are directly related to your player's career, and those that deal with the more personal side of their affairs. Even though negotiating stances vary by each person, there are still certain things that have to be considered when dealing with contracts. Furthermore, it should be noted that taking the advice of a qualified financial advisor or lawyer is also a good idea, and is sometimes a requirement.

Football-related contracts

The following paragraphs make up the most important aspects of a player's footballing contractual agreements.

Representation Contract

In order to legitimately represent a player, there has to be a valid Representation Contract between you and your client as well as, of course, being registered as an intermediary (see Chapter 1 for details). This agreement, which is valid for two years until it needs to be renewed, is an extremely important part of the entire process. The Representation Contract is normally agreed alongside the agent's fee (a certain percentage of the player's salary as agreed by the Employment Contract), and includes a portion of the signing-on fee whilst usually excluding other bonuses like goals or appearances. The recognised norm is that an agent receives 10 per cent of a client's gross salary per year. It is important to note that if the Employment Contract is due to end after the Representation Contract, the intermediary is still entitled to their agreed percentage.

Employment Contract

The contractual relationship between a player and a club is encapsulated in the Employment Contract. This is something that is agreed when the player joins a club (after a transfer), and can be renewed and renegotiated at a later date. The Employment Contract would normally cover a series of different aspects between the two parties – for example, it may include a signing-on bonus as well as appearance or goal bonuses. Here, it would be for the agent of the player to negotiate on their client's behalf, in order to secure the best possible deal. Furthermore, it is crucial for the intermediary to be aware of the rules set out by FIFA and the relevant footballing association regarding contracts, as there are certain criteria that have to be followed and adhered to.

Dual Representation Contract

In most cases, an agent represents the club (for the purposes of the transfer) and the player at the same time, thus leading to an obvious conflict of interests. However, given the inevitability of this conflict, this dual representation is permitted by the footballing associations (again, check the rules for the relevant federation). In order for the agent to be allowed to act on behalf of both parties, they must abide by all the regulations and submit the applicable paperwork. Using the example of England (FA – Football Association), the agent must also sign off on the Tripartite Representation Contract, a document that just confirms the process of dual representation.

Image Rights Agreement

Given the increased commercialisation of sport (especially football), the Image Rights Agreement has become a pivotal part of contract negotiations between club and player. If your client is well known (or has the potential to be a household name) then this part of the contract becomes even more significant. The Image Rights Agreement ensures that the player receives a percentage of the money that the club gains after using their image commercially. Consequently, it would be for the agent to help form a company that would specifically be used to give permission for the rights of a player's image. Again, much like with the Employment Contract, the intermediary would have to check up on the specific rules and regulations regarding the Agreement for the relevant club and association. In some cases, the club will have sold their own image rights to a third party company. Consequently, if a player from this team was to sign a sponsorship agreement, it would be wise (as their agent) to negotiate a deal based on material gifts (and a small fee) rather than a larger cash sum. This would ensure that both you and your client receive the maximum amount from the situation.

Sponsorships – sporting brands

A significant part of a player's (and therefore an agent's) income can come in the form of endorsement deals, particularly with sports brands to wear their football boots as well as clothing. Unlike the strict regulations that come with a Representation Contract, these types of sponsorship deals give the agent more freedom, as there is no maximum percentage cap on the commission. Furthermore, if your player and their club share a common sponsor, it is more likely that your client would become an important part of the advertising campaigns, and this can therefore strengthen your negotiating position when discussing the Image Rights Agreement. However, even if your client's club has a kit sponsor (for example Nike), the player is still allowed to have an endorsement from another brand (like Adidas) to wear their boots and also clothing whilst 'off the pitch'.

Sponsorships – other companies

Although these types of endorsement deals are not specifically linked to football, they are of course only possible due to a player's ability to reach a huge audience as a result of the global nature of the sport. Consequently, sponsorship deals with a range of brands and companies are to be expected. Such deals are normally brought about by the company directly contacting a player's agent, or by the agent being proactive and therefore consciously using their contacts to find potential sponsors. Much like endorsements from sporting brands for boots and clothing, these deals do not have a cap on commission for the agent, thus meaning that they can be really important and lucrative for the intermediary.

Non-football related contracts

The following paragraphs detail some of the more personal aspects of a player's life that an agent could cover, as well as other types of potential deals and endeavours.

Purchase or renting of a property

When a player moves to a club that forces them to change house location, it is often the case that they start by renting a property. This would normally be an area that you, as the agent, would need to sort out and make sure that your client is quickly settled into in order to perform better on the pitch. When your player is in a position to buy a property, it is crucial to be aware of the situation that you find yourself in. If your client is perhaps only on a short-term contract or looking likely to be transferred, it may be better to just rent. On the other hand, if it seems that your client will stay put for a reasonable period of time, it would be beneficial to start searching for a permanent home, which would also act as an investment for the longer term. When dealing with property, it is encouraged to consult a lawyer, especially in countries foreign to you or your client, as property law can vary significantly depending on where you are.

Purchase of a car

This greatly depends on the existing agreements that a client has. If the player already has an endorsement from a car company, for example Mercedes-Benz, it is most likely that the contract would include some sort of arrangement for a car (or even cars) for them. Depending on the exact conditions agreed by the player and their agent, it may forbid them from being seen in public using cars of a different brand. Equally, the contract may involve no such condition. Regardless of the brand of car that the player will eventually have, it still normally remains for the agent to sort out and organise all the details (insurance, services, etc.) that come with having a car.

Charitable agreements

As an agent, it is important to make sure any client is aware of the need to give back to the community, both local and global. Of course, it would be simple for most players to give a donation to any charitable organisation, but it should be thought that their association with the charity (through adverts or campaigns) is also greatly valuable as it can bring worldwide awareness. Furthermore, depending on the 'size' of a client, it could be advantageous to form their own foundation. Obviously, the agent would play a key role in setting up the organisation and be crucial in the administrative and/or legal aspects of its formation. Given the tax exemptions that charitable foundations have, it could be beneficial in that a greater percentage of funds could go directly to those in need, especially if an agent is able to make further deals with existing sponsors to give resources to the newly founded charitable organisation.

Personal business ventures

At the pinnacle of the player's career, it may become possible that potential personal business ventures would be a success. Such a decision is becoming more and more popular amongst top footballers, with many having their own clothing brand, or even chain of hotels! Again, much like for the charitable organisations, it is normally for the agent to help with the administrative side of affairs. The agent should use their contacts to form and sustain a profitable venture, using legal and financial advisors to help make the project effective. In return for this, the agent could receive shares in the company or just take an agreed percentage of revenue. A skilled agent would make sure all personal business ventures are advertised on their client's social media in order to maximise exposure of the brand.

Summary

- Given the legal importance of contracts, it is always advisable to have a strong relationship with a lawyer (or law firm) who you can trust in order to give you impartial guidance and help.
- As the agent, you will play an integral role in every negotiation and agreement that is made with regards to your client – it is therefore crucial that you check over every detail and leave nothing to chance.
- Furthermore, you should always keep your client well informed about every decision that you plan on making, as it is technically on their behalf that you are negotiating.

The expert's view – Daniel Geey (Sports lawyer, Sheridans)

"For high-profile, elite footballers, there are a number of considerations when signing important football-related contracts. Usually, the most significant will be the player's employment contract, image rights deal and boot/apparel agreement. It's vital that a player's agent is negotiating hard to extract the best deal on offer. Similarly, for elite clubs, they will be looking to market the player's image from a retail, TV and commercial partnership perspective. For example, it can be important for the agent finalising the player's boot deal (along with a lawyer) to ensure that if the player is giving away the opportunity to enter into particular deals (because the boot brand agreement covers so many categories), that the player is being rewarded adequately for the deals that they subsequently cannot enter into. The specific products/apparel that a player will be required to wear will include athletic footwear, clothing and accessories like bags, gloves and hats. Such a product list may also cover sunglasses, golf clubs, sports equipment, headphones, personal care and hygiene products, watches and electronic accessories like phone or tablet cases and covers.

"The player will as a result be provided with a variety of branded products to use. The flip side is that the boot deal may actually limit the opportunities for a player to sign additional deals with, say, headphones or watch manufacturers. This is because the boot deal may limit the player to only using their branded products. It's very much down to the agent (along with a lawyer) to guide the player so they are aware that the scope to enter into additional commercial deals may be limited and to work out the best short- to long-term on-field and off-field strategy."

CHAPTER EIGHT

YOUTH POLICIES AND RULES

Intro

Stemming from FIFA regulations, there are very strict rules concerning agents working with youth players and minors. Much like the registration processes (Chapter 1), the football associations all have slightly different rules, yet they are all focused on protecting the young players, with strict punishment (for agents and clubs) if these regulations are not adhered to. With the growth of youth footballing talent around the world leading to more scouts and more transfers, there is increasing monitoring of these policies by football federations.

In recent news, it is clear to see the implications of not following the rules closely. In April 2017, it was reported that Liverpool FC were facing legal action, as well as a ban from signing academy players for over a year and a fine of £100,000 for contacting and allegedly attempting to bribe a schoolboy. Yet such neglect of youth regulations is not confined to England, with Barcelona, Real Madrid and Atlético Madrid all receiving transfer bans in the last few years due to not following the relevant policies. Therefore, these rules have to be followed closely, regardless of the country or association, and make sure that you secure the dates and a copy of any contract signed by a youth player for later reference in case of any disputes of age or legality.

FIFA
(Fédération Internationale de Football Association)

The governing body of football has a fixed set of guidelines regarding minors that must be obeyed by all agents within the 211 member countries:

1. Players can only be transferred internationally over the age of eighteen;
2. The only exceptions (to Rule 1) are those concerning familial, academic or geographical issues – however, a transfer of a player aged sixteen to eighteen can take place within the European Union (EU) or European Economic Area (EEA), whilst arranging education and accommodation;
3. The Players' Status Committee has the power to rule on disputes and impose punishments if these regulations are not abided by.

England
(FA – Football Association)

The rules in relation to intermediaries and youth players in England have recently been updated, and are naturally rigorous. The English footballing body has declared that an agent must not engage in any contact with a player regarding 'intermediary activity' before January 1st of the year which the player will celebrate their sixteenth birthday. This rule is coupled with the fact that any contact with a minor has to be agreed and signed by the player's parent or legal guardian.

Germany
(DFB – Deutscher Fußball-Bund)

In Germany, the rules on the representation of youth players are often thought of as fairly controversial. The more straightforward aspect of this set of regulations is that German labour law instructs that those between seven and eighteen are not eligible to sign a deal without the consent of a parent or legal guardian. Yet the German rules become more complicated with the possibility of signing a *Fördervertrag* – an agreement by both parties (player/ legal guardian and club) to place additional years onto the typical three-year contract. This, of course, goes some way in contradicting the FIFA rules, thus legal ambiguity remains over the issue. Therefore, this stresses the importance of making sure, as the representative of the young player, that you keep all the necessary paperwork and check all the times and dates are correct.

France
(FFF – Fédération Française De Football)

The FFF requires a lawyer or legal consultant to sign the Representation Contract between the agent and the player, if the latter is a minor. In addition, an intermediary may not receive money (or collect any financial rewards) for representing a youth player, and any agent found breaching this rule would be subject to punishment by the federation.

Spain
(RFEF – Real Federación Española de Fútbol)

The RFEF restates the rules given by FIFA in regards to minors. It reiterates how the international transfer of players is only allowed when the player reaches the age of eighteen, yet there are exceptions to this. These exceptions mirror those given earlier in the chapter relating to location, education and accommodation.

Italy
FIGC – Federazione Italiana Giuoco Calcio)

The Italian footballing association details the rights of young players, and has different rules for different age groups. At the age of fourteen, a player can register with a professional club in an arrangement that ties them to it until the end of season commencing the year they turn nineteen (they are the so-called *giovani di serie* players). During the last month of this last season, the player can be hired on a contract that must not exceed three years, but the club which they have been part of since they were fourteen has priority over other clubs. In addition, clubs can offer a **giovane di serie** player an Employment Contract once he turns sixteen. Additionally, players have the right to sign an Employment Contract if a specific number of appearances with the first team have been played. Of course, these rules and regulations have to be followed closely alongside FIFA's rules, and always check the relevant association's website for further clarity.

Portugal
(FPF – Federação Portuguesa de Futebol):

Regarding the relationship between minors and intermediaries, the FPF simply adheres to the rules set out by FIFA. It declares that agents cannot act on behalf of underage athletes. This regulation is reinforced by Portugal's domestic law, which forbids underage representation and exploitation.

United States of America
(USSF – United States Soccer Federation)

The USSF regulations differ slightly to those presented by FIFA. The second aforementioned FIFA ruling (concerning the EU or EEA) is not relevant to the USA given that it is not part of either organisation. Instead, the USSF presents some of its own regulations regarding the transfer of a minor. Depending on the exact situation that the player may find themselves in, the necessary documentation will include birth certificates, proof of parental residence and work, as well as various other papers and records.

Most expensive teenagers (eighteen and under)

Player	Age	Transfer	Fee (M £)
Martin Ødegaard	16	Strømsgodset IF → Real Madrid (Castilla)	£2.52
Theo Walcott	16	Southampton → Arsenal	£9.45
Fabricio Coloccini	17	Boca Juniors → A.C. Milan	£6.75
Gareth Bale	17	Southampton → Tottenham Hotspur	£13.23
Alexandre Pato	17	Internacional → A.C. Milan	£19.8
Antonio Cassano	18	Bari → A.S. Roma	£25.65
Wayne Rooney	18	Everton → Manchester United	£33.3
Luke Shaw	18	Southampton → Manchester United	£33.75
Vinícius Júnior	18	Flamengo → Real Madrid	£40.5
Kylian Mbappé	18	AS Monaco → Paris Saint-Germain	Loan (£166)

Source: *Transfermarkt (correct as of January 2018)*

Summary

- The most crucial point regarding youth rules is to *always* act on the side of caution – the first port of call when trying to find the necessary regulations should be the relevant association's website, and contacting a representative is greatly advised.
- The punishment for not following the rules correctly can be extremely serious – breaking the law, especially when concerning minors, must be avoided.
- Although the FFF (Fédération Française De Football) explicitly calls for a legal representative to oversee the Representation Contract between an agent and minor, it is advised to seek legal consultation in whatever country you are located in to make sure no rules are being breached.

The expert's view – David Jackett (Global Football Consultant, Wasserman)

"Youth football is its own sphere, network and world. The modern game views young players as both low-risk commodities and high quantity 'investments' with the potential of great reward for the successful few.

"A magnifying glass has been placed on youth football like never before, due to amplified worldwide passion from fans. This is coupled with increased access for a supporter to simply be able to follow updates on the other side of the planet. The demand for content overspills to 'who is the next young home-grown star of the team?' This globalised modern world brands young footballers as prospects, ensuring a 'bandwagon' surrounding the next big star from all angles. Millennials have now subconsciously bought into the rising star philosophy through social media. This creates a very different perception to the apprentice reality of today, with old academies being challenged to adapt their teachings in increasingly lucrative and consequently deceptive surroundings. It is this evolution which will not make more players earn a living, but will bring out the best in existing domestic talent who, from the age of twelve, face international competition with more basic upbringings at elite clubs.

"The underbelly of the beautiful game raises questions about each child's journey by writers, coaches, parents and players. Roles are blurred. Injuries occur. Social pressure. Passion overspills. A normal childhood **can** be sacrificed, but the opportunities that come with the prize of success are often far too good to turn down."

CHAPTER NINE

WORKING WITH THE MEDIA

Intro

Despite not normally being closely associated with the important jobs of a football agent, the media (both social media and the press) is something that is pivotal, and when conducted poorly, it can greatly affect a player's reputation and harm the possibility of lucrative sponsorships. The fact that Cristiano Ronaldo has over 275 million social media followers is (in addition to his footballing prowess) a key factor that enables his representatives to strike so many sponsorship deals, as companies know that a single tweet or post can reach a vast and global audience almost immediately. Additionally, the press carries much importance. Although not everything you read in the paper is true, the content that newspapers and news outlets publish still acts as a powerful tool that a good football agent can use to their advantage.

Social media presence

In today's society where social media plays a crucial role and is widely used, it has become vital that a footballer has a good social media presence on the key sites (the table opposite shows the most followed and liked football players). It is crucial to have popular social media pages as it allows the player to increase their global reach and in turn be able to better negotiate potential sponsorship deals. It is common for either the agent to control the social media of the player, or (for perhaps more famous clients) organise a digital agency to take care of the accounts and posts. In both situations, it is important that the messages given to fans are positive (for example, posting a picture of the player working hard at training or in the gym) and also conform to contractual agreements with the club and sponsors. For example, a company may sponsor the player to wear their sportswear, and the contract states that there is to be a minimum of five posts with that brand in a month. Therefore, it is of great significance that the social media accounts are well organised and dealt with.

Player	Instagram (M)	Facebook (M)	Twitter (M)	Overall (M)
Cristiano Ronaldo	119.7	122.6	68.4	310.7
Neymar Jr.	119.7	60.8	37.3	186.1
Lionel Messi	88.0	89.5	0.0	175.9
James Rodríguez	86.4	32.9	15.7	83.1
Gareth Bale	34.5	28.8	16.1	77.3
Andrés Iniesta	32.4	27.0	21.2	69.0
Mesut Özil	15.1	31.5	21.2	67.8
Zlatan Ibrahimović	29.9	26.6	4.8	61.3
Sergio Ramos	21.2	23.5	13.8	58.5
Luis Suárez	26.0	19.0	13.2	58.2

Sources: Instagram, Facebook, Twitter (correct as of January 2018)

Things *not* to do on social media!

Given the importance of social media in regards to the success of an agent's player 'off the pitch', it is crucial to remember that there are many things to consider when posting and certain things are simply **not** to be done.

Avoid:

1. Being critical of anybody, regardless of whether it is connected to football – this can be bad for relations with sponsorships and can jeopardise existing or future deals;

2. Discussing injuries and tactics – this can give opponents an advantage;

3. Posting messages consisting of 'sensitive' material – this includes anything that could cause offence (ranging from indecent photos to a controversial political stance);

4. Posting something that is inaccurate or done out of frustration – again this could isolate sponsors and create a 'bad image'.

The press

A common term for mainstream media (newspapers and news outlets), the press is another key area which a successful football agent must be aware of and know how to use to their players' (and therefore their own) advantage. Clearly, not everything in the papers is true, yet the power of rumours is really important when it concerns the transfer or contract of a player. If an agent has good connections and links into mainstream media outlets (like a popular newspaper), it is greatly beneficial as their work can be used to put pressure on clubs to adhere to an agent's demands due to fan speculation. For example, if you're looking for a new contract for your client, an article that describes the importance of them for their club can improve your negotiating stance as a result of fans agreeing and putting pressure on the board or manager.

Interviews and media work

Within social media and the press, interviews are a great way to boost the popularity of a player as well as impress existing and future sponsors. Interviews can take place in a number of different forms, and in cases where an agent cannot be present (for example a pre- or post-match interview with the club), it is crucial that the intermediary tells their player how to conduct themselves in an appropriate way.

The other common types of interview occur either on social media (perhaps as a live Instagram or Facebook session or a Twitter Q&A) or as a feature article in a mainstream news outlet. It is the agent's responsibility (or in some cases the appointed digital agency) to have prior knowledge of the questions to ensure that the interview goes smoothly and depicts the player in a positive light. This is why having last authorisation on the questions, as well as the power to dictate the article headline, is of paramount importance. Although interviews are frequently beneficial, it is crucial not to accept every invitation. This is because with each interview, the exclusivity of your player's comments or story will slightly reduce – therefore it is recommended that the agent chooses perhaps the most well-known newspapers or interviewers in order to attract the biggest audiences.

Global sporting news outlets

Country	Sports news outlets
England	BBC Sport, Sky Sports, *FourFourTwo* magazine
Germany	*Bild, Kicker*
France	*L'Équipe, France Football*
Spain	*Marca, AS, Sport, Estadio Deportivo*
Italy	*La Gazzetta dello Sport, Corriere dello Sport, Tuttosport*
Portugal	*A Bola, O Jogo, Record*
USA	*ESPN, Bleacher Report, Sports Illustrated*

This list is of course not exhaustive, and most mainstream newspapers have their own influential sports columns that are widely read. When choosing which news outlets would be most beneficial for your player to interview with, it is important to consider the audience which the organisation appeals to, in conjunction with the country or regions that it sells in.

Working with journalists

Knowing which journalists to trust is something that all agents find difficult at some point, and is a part of the profession that you pick up as you go along! As an agent, you will always get calls asking about the future of your clients, with many journalists phrasing the questions in a clever and manipulative way. Therefore, you always have to be cautious, as any mistake could be costly. However, this doesn't mean that you should not pursue any relations with journalists, as they can be greatly effective in strengthening your stance as an agent representing a client.

Summary

- Both social media and the press carry great significance, and work in this field has to be conducted effectively and smartly.
- Whether or not a digital agency takes care of your client's social media, it remains crucial for the agent to be highly involved and have the final say on everything that is posted – remember, once it has been put online, there is no going back.
- Much like every other aspect of the profession, you should make sure your client is aware of everything that relates to media and outreach, as they will have their own ideas about how they want to be presented to the public.

The expert's view – Rory Smith (Chief Soccer Correspondent, *New York Times*)

"Nothing is quite so treasured by a football journalist as a strong, open, trusting relationship with an agent. That is no surprise. Journalism's prime currency is information, and there are few quite so rich in that as agents. They know if their clients are happy to stay or about to leave a club; they know which players are complaining about the manager and which remain loyal; they have their fingers on the pulse of what is happening throughout the game. Being able to share information with an agent should be the perfect way to make our work more accurate.

"It does not always work like that. As a rule, journalists encounter three types of agents. The best are those who are willing to trust you, to offer an honest reflection of reality as they see it. Second are those who do not engage at all, who will not answer the phone, or simply offer a gruff 'no comment'. And third are those who, believing you need them more than they need you, choose to distort the truth to further their own ends.

"Even at a time when many players prefer to access their fans directly through social media, there are increasingly few of the latter group. More and more agents recognise that journalists are not the enemy. In an age when players are as much brands as athletes, the media can help to present a true reflection of their clients; they can get their side of the story out in such a way that it does not look like propaganda; they can boost their profile. The cost is not high: just honest answers to a few questions every now and again."

CHAPTER TEN

HISTORY OF THE PROFESSION

Intro

Perhaps not thought of as a profession that has much history, the football agent industry does in fact have a fairly rich as well as an intriguing past. Given how the sport has gone from not needing agents to heavily relying on them in everyday practices, the rapid increase in importance is in large part due to the advancements made in the mid-1990s. During this time, agents were to become officially recognised by FIFA, and the crucial court case that took place in 1995 (the 'Bosman ruling') completely revolutionised the business. Nevertheless, the roots of this business began well before this date, and can be traced back to the late 1800s when certain aspects of intermediary activity are evident.

The early stages

During the nineteenth century there was really no such thing as a football agent, although this did not stop J.P. Campbell from submitting an article to the English newspaper **Athletic News** looking for young footballing talent in 1891. Nevertheless, despite Campbell's publication, the active participation of an intermediary regarding a transfer and contract was unheard of. Decades later in the 1930s, it was clear that football was having to reflect the politics and international relations of the era, with nearly all the major European football associations placing limits (or even bans) on the transfer of foreign players. Whilst the FFF (Fédération Française De Football) fought hard to counter these decisions, the very concept of a football agent was in doubt as it heavily relied upon the prospect of transfers which were sparse at this time. However, hope for intermediaries still existed in Europe, and similarities to today can be pinpointed. In Italy, the establishment of a transfer market gave birth to talks between club owners and directors, as well as intermediaries, with such discussions over players often taking place at the Gallia Hotel in Milan. Therefore, it is clear that this was a time where intermediary activity was festering, yet in general the agency profession was mostly limited.

Representation of football players

Despite there being strict regulations regarding transfers, and therefore agents, the desire across Europe to create better football clubs, coupled with increasing political cooperation post-World War II, started to enable the growth of prominent intermediaries. The first of this new breed of well-known agents was Gigi Peronace, who specialised in transfers between the English and Italian leagues. He played a key role in many ground-breaking deals at the time, including John Charles (Leeds United to Juventus), Jimmy Greaves (Chelsea to A.C. Milan) and Denis Law (Manchester City to Torino), earning him notability and success.

Years later, agents started to understand the commercial opportunities that their clients could receive with their fame. After his transfer to Hamburg in 1977, Keegan and his representatives signed football's first 'face deal'. This contract, nowadays known as an Image Rights Agreement, enabled him to become one of the most instantly recognisable celebrities by promoting any product that came his way. Consequently, Keegan quickly became a valuable asset for any agent, and set the precedent for future deals and proceedings.

Recognition by FIFA

With football agents becoming more and more prominent within the sport, it was inevitable that formal recognition was eventually going to happen. In 1994, FIFA finally implemented the first set of rules and regulations regarding football agents, which in turn made football agency a formal profession. This meant that football federations across the world now had guidelines about how to become a licensed agent, thus heralding the beginning of the modern intermediary, whose role and power greatly increased within the sport.

The 'Bosman ruling'

Whilst 1994 was clearly a pivotal year for football agents, the following year, 1995, was equally important, as the 'Bosman ruling' would shape the way football worked and still plays a crucial part in the sport today. The court ruling meant that a player could move club without their former team receiving a transfer fee. As a result, due to the lack of transfer fee, agents could demand larger salaries for their clients and, consequently, larger commissions for themselves. An example of this can be seen just four years after the rule was implemented. Steve McManaman became the highest-paid British footballer at the time when he moved to Real Madrid from Liverpool at the end of his contract. This way of thinking remains exactly the same today, with 'free agents' (as they are now called) a very common method of transfer that is often exploited by intermediaries. The following table gives some famous examples of the 'Bosman ruling' being carried out.

Player	Country	Year	Transfer
Edgar Davids	Netherlands	1996	Ajax → A.C. Milan
Steve McManaman	England	1999	Liverpool → Real Madrid
Brad Friedel	United States of America	2000	Tottenham Hotspur → Blackburn
Sol Campbell	England	2001	Tottenham Hotspur → Arsenal
Henrik Larsson	Sweden	2004	Celtic → Barcelona
Esteban Cambiasso	Argentina	2004	Real Madrid → Inter Milan
Michael Ballack	Germany	2006	Bayern Munich → Chelsea
David Beckham	England	2007	Real Madrid → LA Galaxy
Andrea Pirlo	Italy	2011	A.C. Milan → Juventus
Robert Lewandowski	Poland	2014	Borussia Dortmund → Bayern Munich
Zlatan Ibrahimović	Sweden	2016	Paris Saint-Germain → Manchester United

Source: Transfermarkt (correct as of January 2018)

Summary

- Although knowing about the history of the profession is not a prerequisite for success in the industry, the past is something that all football agents have in common.

- It is clear that events in the mid-1990s were pivotal in the creation of the modern intermediary, as football agency was given both recognition and power.
- The 'Bosman ruling' paved the way for a type of transfer that gives agents the advantage over clubs when a player's contract is coming to the end, with such cases being pertinent to this day.

The expert's view – Jörg Neubauer (Agent of Leon Goretzka and Kevin Trapp)

"I started working in the field of football agency in 1990, at a time where the profession was simply limited to helping broker deals. However, during that time I began to understand that a player needs more than just someone who could negotiate a contract. As a result, I started to learn about areas such as tax and insurance, legal advice, public relations and press activities – many of which seem like relative necessities for the agency business. For me, this was the step towards the professionalisation of player consulting. In addition, it was clear that there was a huge transformation occurring – something which I describe as the 'transparency of footballers'. Through the internet, social media and data collection, there is absolutely no room for secrets anymore. Nowadays, everything is public and easy to access – this represents the most fundamental shift and transition of the business over the last twenty-five years.

"The football market has always been interesting and the game of football itself has had its own individual development ongoing. Nevertheless, the greatest steps taken have not been towards sporting success, but rather regarding monetary terms. The huge increase in commercialisation within football, especially through the increased income outside of the stadium (such as broadcasting rights and sponsorships) means there is more money available. Consequently, this has led to the aforementioned change in the nature of football agency. Whereas during the 1990s an agent was an individual, today agencies are in the majority, and this has somewhat led to the disappearance of the individual within the industry. As a pioneer in this field I started to establish a scouting network for young players at the end of the 1990s, and with a scout I was able to find the best talents. This area also shows a rapid development. Similar to football clubs, the agencies started to build their own national as well as international scouting systems. The result was that the growth of a player started much younger.

"Summing up, this business has gone through an enormous transition since I started. Despite this, one thing has remained a constant in all these years – the agent who represents the best players is the agent who does the best business."

CHAPTER ELEVEN

'SHOW ME THE MONEY'

Intro

Like any profession, money is always a crucial factor when deciding whether to pursue it or not. The positive thing with football is that there is certainly no shortage of money! The transfer of Neymar Jr. to Paris Saint-Germain from Barcelona for £200m shows that clubs are willing to pay whatever it takes to increase their own chances of winning and of success. Consequently, given the growing importance of agents in the sport, there is certainly the possibility of earning yourself a living.

Wages

As detailed in Chapter 7, your constant source of income comes from the Representation Contract that you have agreed with your client. This entitles you to around 10 per cent of the player's gross annual salary, and is normally paid to you by the club itself. Although a small percentage of someone else's wages seems like a bad deal, football is like no other profession! It is estimated that the total European wage bill for footballers is around £9.5 billion per year and thus there is certainly room for you to take a slice of this huge and growing market. Using all the skills and connections that you would have formed, it is up to you to negotiate your client the best possible deal, and in turn make yourself more money.

Transfers

With wages offering you a steady flow of money, transfers provide an alternative source of income for you as an agent. Whether you have a mandate for a player's transfer or you are their registered agent (this difference is noted in Chapter 4) there is potential to make a large sum of money when your client moves club. More often than not, the transfer includes a set fee for the agent as a commission for brokering the deal. This was highlighted by the sum paid to Paul Pogba's agent, Mino Raiola, for his work during the £89m transfer from Juventus to Manchester United during the summer of 2016. Although this particular case demonstrates an extreme, it is certainly true that agent fees are rising, with more and more clubs willing to pay intermediaries due to their role in transfers for their clients. Such a notion is evidenced in the table on the next page, with Premier League clubs spending just under £175m on combined agents' fees in the 2016–17 season.

Club	Total agents' fees (2016–17)
Arsenal	£10,156,567
Bournemouth	£7,415,321
Burnley	£2,567,268
Chelsea	£25,051,431
Crystal Palace	£5,998,074
Everton	£5,081,134
Hull City	£1,916,525
Leicester City	£5,359,409
Liverpool	£13,792,355
Manchester City	£26,286,998
Manchester United	£19,000,973
Middlesbrough	£2,478,379
Southampton	£6,321,036
Stoke City	£5,442,113
Sunderland	£5,833,611
Swansea City	£4,330,533
Tottenham Hotspur	£7,167,773
Watford	£6,292,751
West Bromwich Albion	£4,248,605
West Ham United	£9,486,397

Source: BBC Sport

Sponsorship and endorsement deals

A crucial source of income that an agent has to make the most of is commercial deals. This area is greatly linked to the Image Rights Agreement (see Chapter 7) and has to be conducted in a professional and smart manner. As a primary decision-maker in the business side of your player's career, you could decide to sell their marketing rights to a firm. This deal would involve a minimum guarantee for all parties and contractual obligations over the splitting of any revenue. Of course, it is your responsibility to go to these companies with presentations and ideas, whilst utilising your network to help 'open the doors' and get in touch with the right people.

Other projects

Another way in which an agent can make money is through other projects, which are inherently linked with their existing clients. Due to the power and attraction that football players have, they can easily open doors for agents to pursue further business ventures. For example, it is not uncommon for agents, along with their client's resources, to create a clothing brand or perhaps open up a restaurant. Starting an additional business with a football player gives you a social media platform of potentially millions of fans for instant advertising, as well as the prospect of getting wealthy partners to join the project.

Summary

- Whilst it shouldn't be the main motivating factor, the money available for you to make by being an intermediary is enticing and by no means unrealistic.
- The commission that you receive from representing a client *can* be your only source of income, but not

capitalising on the business opportunities that stem from the player's popularity is a missed opportunity.

- Yet there is a strong distinction to be made between good business and simply taking advantage of your player's fame and wealth – you ought to be open, honest and transparent, as well as always incorporating your client within the business, if you decide to pursue 'off-the-pitch' work.

The expert's view – Pere Guardiola (Director, Media Base Sports)

"I am fortunate enough to have had the opportunity of working in the sports business for many years now. One of the most important things that you should know is that football is such a big industry and the possibilities of making money are endless. So if you don't have contacts to get you an internship at a large agency, or a friend who is playing professionally, it doesn't matter.

"There are many ways to make a successful living in the football industry. Of course, there are the better-known methods as already mentioned in this book such as transfers (where you can work on either the club or player side – or in some cases both) as well as commercial deals for your client. Additionally, there are further opportunities relating to football itself such as M&A (mergers and acquisitions), where you can use the network you have to put together a club looking to sell and an investor looking to buy, taking a percentage of the total sale as your commission or introductory fee.

"Moreover, away from the pitch, you can advise your

client(s) on investments in a range of industries, including, for example, restaurants and coffee shops. Subsequently, you would be entitled to take a share in the business as your commission. The same can also be said for property and other tangible investments.

"Remember, the opportunities that present themselves to you in this business are extremely valuable. Take them and use them wisely, then the money will come to *you*!"

CONCLUSION

Football agency is a tough business that ultimately requires you to be hard-working, flexible and hungry for success – it demands sacrifice and diligence from the start. At first, this can seem daunting and unattainable, but at the same time, the challenges you face should act as greater motivation. No profession allows you to rise to the top with immediate effect, and this industry is no different. Nevertheless, with the increased professionalisation of football and intermediaries, there is every possibility that you can leave your mark on the game. Whilst this job is certainly competitive, there is no shortage of football players to represent, and the future will only pave the way for a greater role for agents.

There is no hiding from the hard work and number of hours needed to succeed in this business, but at the same time one must not neglect the perks of the job. Being involved in the world's most popular sport and mixing with football players often entitles you to unforgettable experiences across the globe that are unparalleled in the majority of other industries. Additionally, as mentioned in Chapter 11, the money in football can allow you to be well remunerated throughout your career. However, although money is a key consideration, it **cannot** be the aspect of the job that motivates you from the outset. Like nearly all professions when starting out, the money simply isn't there, as experience and clients will be lacking. This is why perseverance and passion have to be characteristics that you possess – having qualities such as these gives you the greatest chance at success.

Of paramount importance to remember is the notion of not giving up. If you decided to embark on a career in football agency, it will be difficult and at times feel impossible – but by working hard and working smart, there is nothing stopping you from achieving the goals that you have set yourself.

SOCIAL MEDIA

Get in touch for more information on becoming a football agent:

Website **www.footballagenteduation.com**
Instagram **@footballagenteducation**
Facebook **Football Agent Education**
Twitter **@education_agent**